Exploring The Great Pyramid of Giza

One of the Seven Wonders of the World

History Kids Books
Children's Ancient History

BABY PROFESSOR
EDUCATION KIDS

In this book, we're going to talk about the Great Pyramid of Giza. So, let's get right to it!

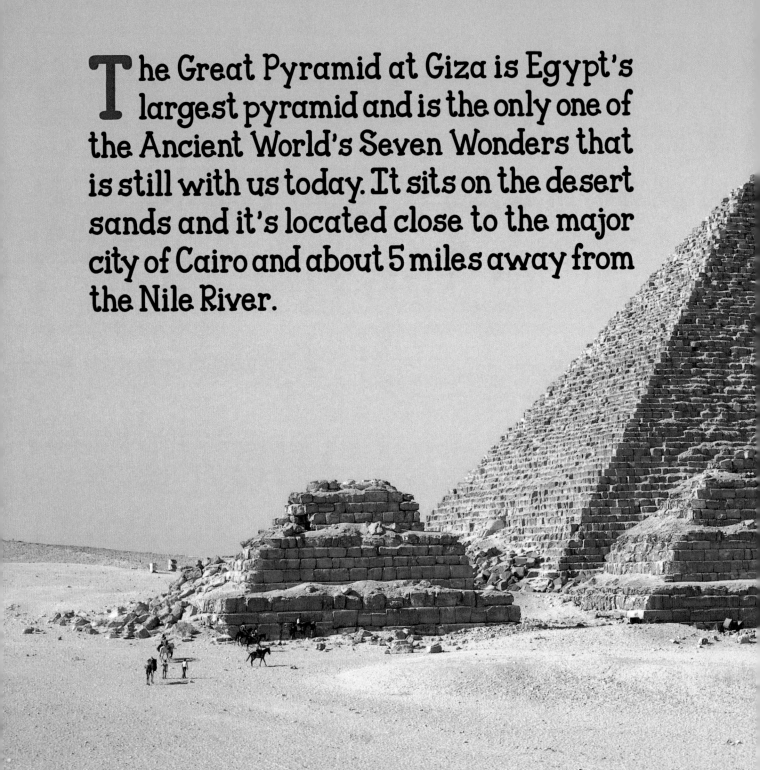

The Great Pyramid at Giza is Egypt's largest pyramid and is the only one of the Ancient World's Seven Wonders that is still with us today. It sits on the desert sands and it's located close to the major city of Cairo and about 5 miles away from the Nile River.

ARCHAEOLOGISTS

It is one of the most famous structures from the time of ancient civilizations. In fact, today archaeologists are still baffled as to how this amazing building could have been built in that time period. It wasn't the first pyramid, but in terms of its size and the accuracy of the measurements that were required to built it, it is the most incredible. Even with our modern building techniques of today, it would be difficult if not impossible to create a building like the Great Pyramid.

HOW OLD IS THE PYRAMID AND HOW LONG DID IT TAKE TO BUILD?

Shortly after the Pharaoh Khufu came to power, construction began on the pyramid in 2580 BC. The architect who created the design for the pyramid was more than likely Khufu's vizier whose name was Hemiunu. He was the second in command. Today the pyramid is almost 4600 years old!

THE PYRAMID OF GIZA

THE CONSTRUCTION OF THE PYRAMID

The construction was finished around 2560 BC, which means it took about 20 years for the pyramid to be built. Archaeologists estimate that it took a workforce of at least 20,000 workers and possibly as many as 100,000 in order to complete the construction within that 20 years.

For many years it was believed that slaves were enlisted to do this work. However, recent evidence shows that the skilled laborers who built the pyramid were paid.

HOW MANY STONES ARE IN THE PYRAMID?

Over 2 million stone blocks were used to construct the Great Pyramid of Giza. It's estimated that each block weighs an average of 2.5 to 15 tons! There was no cement or mortar to keep the stones together. The stones have been shaped to fit together so perfectly that not even a slip of paper can be wedged between them.

The sides of the Great Pyramid at Giza aren't stepped like some of the other pyramids in Egypt. Instead, they are flat. However, it wasn't noticed until an aviator flew over the pyramid in 1940 and took photographs, that the sides are actually slightly concave.

This engineering technique prevented the blocks from slipping off each other. This means that each of the pyramid's four sides is actually two sides that are bent a little toward each other.

WHY WAS THE GREAT PYRAMID BUILT?

The Great Pyramid was constructed to be Khufu's tomb. As with all burials done by the Egyptians, the tomb was designed to hold the Pharaoh's coffin, which was called a sarcophagus, as well as all the other items he would need in the afterlife. The pyramid contained three different chambers that were designed for burials of some type.

Sarcophagus of Egyptian Priest Hornedjitef

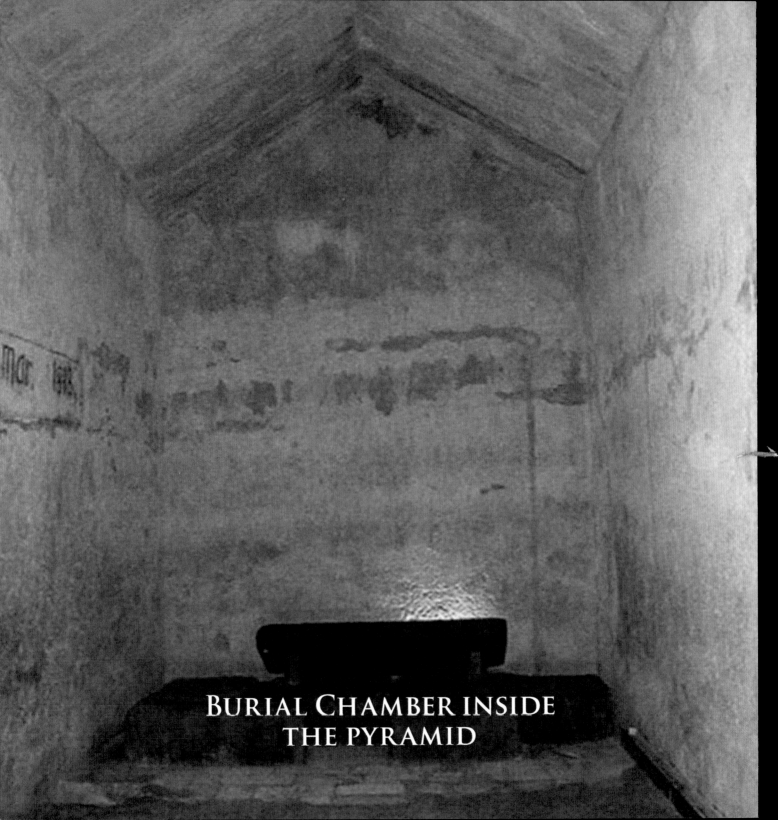

BURIAL CHAMBER INSIDE
THE PYRAMID

The first of these chambers is completely underground and was carved out from bedrock. The second chamber was above ground and was originally thought to be the chamber for the Pharaoh's main wife, but later evidence showed that this was not the case.

It's believed now that this second chamber was for a statue of the king that had special spiritual significance. The third of the chambers was for the Pharaoh's body and held a sarcophagus, made of red granite. It was designed so that the Pharaoh's sarcophagus would be positioned in the pyramid's exact center.

There were air shafts built from these chambers to the outside. Workers on the inside would have needed oxygen to work inside the pyramid.

ABU SIMBEL STATUE

PHARAOHS BURIAL CHAMBER

THE GRAND GALLERY

Explorers eventually found a mysterious passageway that led to an architectural masterpiece. The slanted passageway was less than 7 feet in width, but more than 150 feet long and almost 29 feet tall. The walls were constructed from enormous blocks of granite that came from the stone quarry at Aswan. The walkway was empty of decoration and there were no artifacts. This was the walkway that led to the Pharaoh's burial chamber.

This passageway is called the Grand Gallery and it has an amazing ceiling. The ceiling is a type of construction called a corbelled arch. This type of arch has stones that are stacked on top of each other with just a slight overhang of about 3 inches.

PHARAOHS BURIAL CHAMBER

The top meets at a peak. Each layer of blocks holds the layer below it in place. There are seven layers of rock in the Gallery. The granite slabs that were used in the Grand Gallery each weigh as much as 50 tons. The visual effect and the technology of this arch is incredible.

These types of vaults exist in both Mayan temples as well as some ancient ruins in Ireland, however the Grand Gallery is one of the oldest examples ever found. At one point, there were sliding granite pieces to seal off the Grand Gallery from thieves but somehow the tomb was raided anyway because in modern times, no treasures have been found inside the tomb.

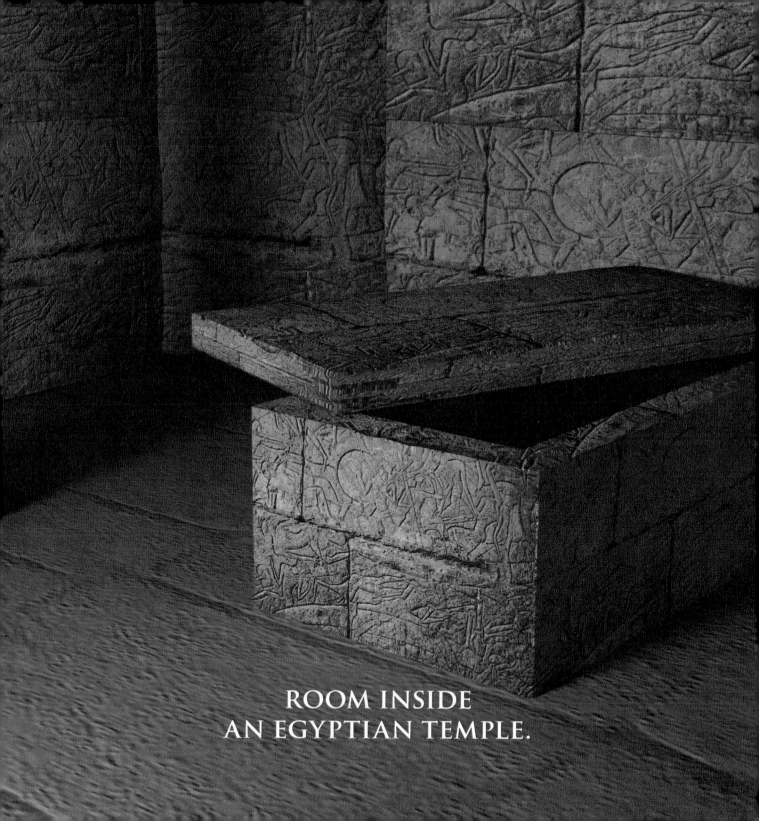

ROOM INSIDE
AN EGYPTIAN TEMPLE.

It's thought that it was looted thousands of years ago. Some archaeologists believe that the three chambers that have been found are just to deceive tomb raiders and that there is a fourth chamber holding all the treasures that still reside within the pyramid.

There are low ramps on each side of the Gallery. There are exactly twenty-seven notches in the side walls that match up with twenty-seven square-shaped holes in the ramp. Some archaeologists believe that wooden beams were positioned in these openings to move building materials up the slope.

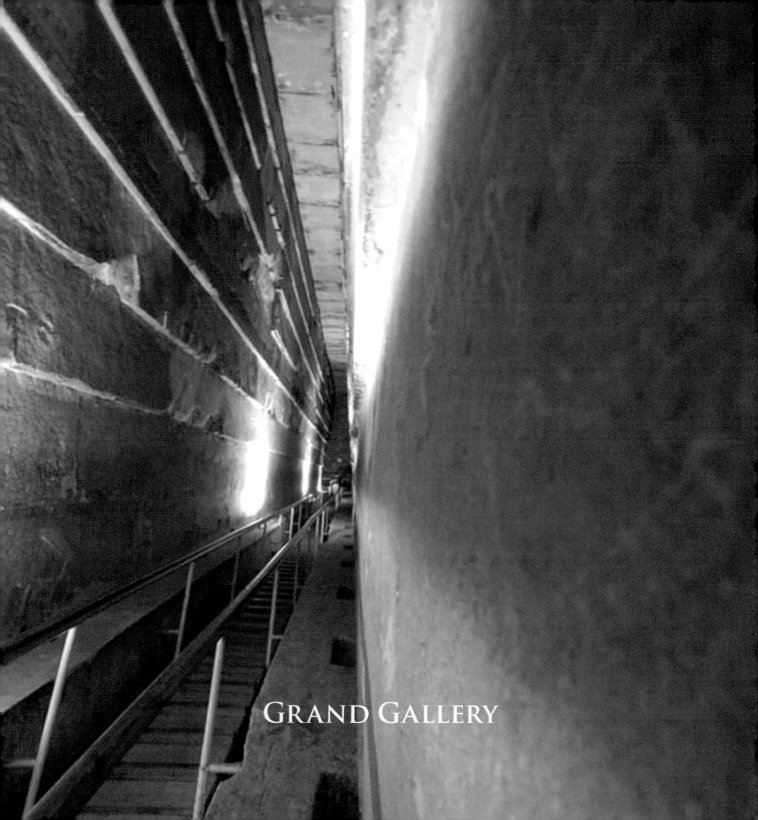

GRAND GALLERY

INTERIOR OF A PYRAMID

Another possibility is that they were used to support the enormous blocks while the stonemasons were building the ceiling. Yet another suggested possibility is that they supported stone blocks that were the roof of the passage to the Queen's Chamber. These same blocks would also have acted as a floor for the Gallery to the passageway that ascended into the King's chamber.

THE ESCAPE SHAFT

In the Great Gallery there is a mysterious opening in the west wall just above the door. It's called the escape shaft and it leads to a hallway deep under the pyramid and to the entrance to the chambers that are underground.

The Escape Shaft

There are some very rough holes in the shaft that look like they were cut there so that men who were building inside could escape. The workers would need a way to get out once the blocks had been lowered into the slanted corridor when the burial ceremony was completed.

However, this purpose isn't known with 100% certainty. After all, couldn't the shaft have been filled from above once the burial was complete? It seems unlikely that they wouldn't close it. Another possibility was that the Egyptians had continuing ceremonies in the burial chambers and needed some way to access them.

PASSAGE

YOUNG EXPLORERS

Some archaeologists have suggested that this special shaft could have been needed to provide air to workers who were digging underground. However, this theory doesn't seem to work either since it's assumed that those chambers would have been the very first stage in the process of construction. Perhaps we'll never fully know the mystery behind the escape shaft.

HOW BIG IS THE PYRAMID?

When the Great Pyramid was constructed, its height was about 481 feet tall. Today, due to erosion, the pyramid is about 455 feet tall. Each side of the base runs about 750 feet in length. That's over twice the length of a football field!

LINCOLN CATHEDRAL

For over 3,800 years it was the tallest structure worldwide until in 1300 AD a spire was placed on the top of England's Lincoln Cathedral.

The base of the pyramid takes up about 13 acres of land. Originally, the entire pyramid was covered with polished pieces of limestone.

This smooth white limestone would have shined in the sun making it appear almost as if the pyramid had a mirrored surface. Unfortunately, these cover stones were removed to be used for other buildings over the years.

THE GIZA NECROPOLIS

The Great Pyramid is part of a larger group of tombs–the Giza Necropolis. A necropolis is essentially a huge area of land that is devoted to burial chambers. There are two other main pyramids in this necropolis. The Pyramid of Khafre, is the middle pyramid and was built for Khufu's son. The pyramid located at the southernmost location at Giza was built for the grandson of Khufu and the son of Khafre. His name was Menkaure.

Pyramid of Khafre

GREAT SPHINX OF GIZA

Another part of Khafre's burial complex is the statue of the Great Sphinx. This enormous statue has the head of a man on top of a lion's body. It was the ancient world's largest statue at 240 feet in length and 66 feet tall. Eventually, this incredible monument was worshipped as another form of Horus, the god of the sky.

There were also three smaller pyramids lined up next to the Great Pyramid. These were the tombs designed for Khufu's wives. Khufu's pyramid is encircled by mastabas, which were rectangular burial chambers for the government officials who would go with him and help him in the afterlife.

Pyramid of Djoser

Awesome! Now you know more about the Great Pyramid of Giza, one of the Ancient World's Seven Wonders. You can find more Ancient History books from Baby Professor by searching the website of your favorite book retailer.

Visit

BABY PROFESSOR
EDUCATION KIDS

www.BabyProfessorBooks.com

to download Free Baby Professor eBooks
and view our catalog of new and exciting
Children's Books

Made in the USA
Las Vegas, NV
29 April 2024

89267103R00040